Conflict Resolution for Holy Beings

ALSO BY JOY HARJO

Crazy Brave: A Memoir

Soul Talk, Song Language: Conversations with Joy Harjo

For a Girl Becoming

She Had Some Horses

How We Became Human: New and Selected Poems

A Map to the Next World

The Good Luck Cat

Reinventing the Enemy's Language: Contemporary Native Women's Writing of North America

The Spiral of Memory

The Woman Who Fell from the Sky

Fishing

In Mad Love and War

Secrets from the Center of the World

What Moon Drove Me to This?

The Last Song

 JOY HARJO

Conflict Resolution for Holy Beings

 *Poems*

W. W. Norton & Company ✕ NEW YORK | LONDON

For information about permission to reproduce selections from
this book, write to Permissions, W. W. Norton & Company, Inc.,
500 Fifth Avenue, New York, NY 10110

For information about special discounts for bulk purchases,
please contact W. W. Norton Special Sales at
specialsales@wwnorton.com or 800-233-4830

Manufacturing by RR Donnelley Westford
Book design by Brooke Koven
Production manager: Louise Mattarelliano

Library of Congress Cataloging-in-Publication Data

Harjo, Joy.
[Poems. Selections]
Conflict resolution for holy beings : poems / Joy Harjo. — First
edition.
pages ; cm
ISBN 978-0-393-24850-0 (hardcover)
I. Title.
PS3558.A62423A6 2015
811'.54—dc23

2015013921

W. W. Norton & Company, Inc., 500 Fifth Avenue,
New York, N.Y. 10110
www.wwnorton.com

W. W. Norton & Company Ltd., Castle House, 75/76 Wells
Street, London W1T 3QT

1 2 3 4 5 6 7 8 9 0

Bless the poets, the workers for justice,
the dancers of ceremony, the singers of heartache,
the visionaries, all makers and carriers of fresh
meaning— We will all make it through,
despite politics and wars, despite failures
and misunderstandings. There is only love.

FOR OWEN CHOPOKSA SAPULPA

Contents

Acknowledgments

"I am sitting in the dark . . ." Desiray Chee. Permission of the author.

"The sound of cicadas as I lay here waiting for sleep . . ." Haleigh Sarah Bush. Permission of author.

"How it came to be . . ." Phillip Deere, *Akwesasne Notes*, Summer 1978, Rooseveltown, NY.

"Rabbit Is Up to Tricks," CD, *Winding Through the Milky Way*, Mekko Productions Inc., 2008; *Black Renaissance Noire*, vol. 9, no. 1, Winter 2009; *Little Patuxent Review*, Columbia, MD, Summer 2009; *Crazy Brave*, W. W. Norton, NY, 2012; *Seeds of Fire: Contemporary Poetry from the Other USA*, Jon Anderson, Smokestack Books, 2014.

"No," *Poets Against the War*, Sam Hamill, Nation Books, NY, 2003; *World Literature Today*, July 2007; *Beloit Poetry Journal*, *Split This Rock Chapbook*, vol. 58, no. 3, Spring 2008; http://www.thedrunkenboat.com/harjo.html.

"Humans were created . . ." from *A Map to the Next World*, W. W. Norton, NY, 2001.

"Once the World Was Perfect," Joy Harjo, *Wings of Night Sky, Wings of Morning Light* (play), 2013 ; *Crazy Brave*, W. W. Norton, NY, 2012.

"We Were There When Jazz Was Invented," published as

"Letter to Lawson," *The Kenyon Review*, vol. XXVIII, Summer 2006.

"Reality Show," *Native Joy for Real*, Mekko Productions Inc., 2004; *Under the Rock Umbrella: Contemporary Poets from 1951 to 1977*, edited by William Walsh, Mercer University Press, Macon, GA, 2006; *Poetic Voices Without Borders 2*, Robert C. Giron, Gival Press, Arlington, VA, 2009.

"Beautiful Baby, Beautiful Child," translation by Rosemary McCombs Maxey.

"Talking with the Sun," *This I Believe*, Holt Paperbacks, 2007; *Cutthroat, A Journal of the Arts*, vol. 4, Spring 2008.

"Mother Field," *Under the Rock Umbrella: Contemporary Poets from 1951 to 1977*, edited by William Walsh, Mercer University Press, Macon, GA, 2006.

"Walk," "Water spirit feeling . . . round my head . . ." from "Witchi Tai To," Jim Pepper.

"Had-It-Up-to-Here Round Dance," *Native Joy for Real*, Mekko Productions Inc., 2004.

"Goin' Home," *Winding Through the Milky Way*, Mekko Productions Inc., 2008.

"Falling, Falling," Joy Harjo, *Wings of Night Sky, Wings of Morning Light* (play), 2013.

"Listening to Blues in a Fish Joint, Downtown Denver," *Crazy Brave*, W. W. Norton, NY, 2012.

"Indian School Night Song Blues," Joy Harjo, *Wings of Night Sky, Wings of Morning Light* (play), 2013.

"This Morning I Pray for My Enemies," *The Massachusetts Review*, "Celebrating Fifty Years," Spring/Summer 2009, Amherst, MA, 2009; *Beloit Poetry Journal*; *Cutthroat, A Journal of the Arts*, vol. 4, Spring 2008.

"I am the holy being of my mother's prayer and my father's

song," Norman Patrick Brown, Facebook post. Used by permission of Norman Patrick Brown.

"I Am Not Ready to Die Yet," *How We Became Human: New and Selected Poems*, W. W. Norton, NY, 2004; http://www.the drunkenboat.com/harjo.html.

"Report from the Edge of a Terrible Regime," *The Más Tequila Review*, Winter 2011, no. 2, Albuquerque, NM, 2011.

"The Last World of Fire and Trash," CD, *Native Joy for Real*, Mekko Productions Inc., 2004; *Poetic Voices Without Borders 2*, Robert C. Giron, Gival Press, Arlington, VA, 2009; http://www.molossus.co/worldpoetryportfolio/world-poetry -portfolio-36-joy-harjo/.

"You Can Change the Story, My Spirit Said to Me . . ." *The Power of Dreaming*, Susan Morgan, CreateSpace independent publishing platform, 2011.

"Sunrise Healing Song," Joy Harjo, *Wings of Night Sky, Wings of Morning Light* (play), 2013.

"It's Raining in Honolulu," *How We Became Human: New and Selected Poems*, W. W. Norton, NY, 2004; *World Literature Today*, July 2007; *Beloit Poetry Journal, Split This Rock Chapbook*, vol. 58, no. 3, Spring 2008; http://www.molossus.co/ worldpoetryportfolio/world-poetry-portfolio-36-joy-harjo/; http://www.thedrunkenboat.com/harjo.html.

"Time is a being . . ." Joy Harjo, *Wings of Night Sky, Wings of Morning Light* (play), 2013.

"Rushing the *Pali*," *How We Became Human: New and Selected Poems*, W. W. Norton, NY, 2004; http://www.thedrunkenboat .com/harjo.html.

"Everybody Has a Heartache," *Poetry Magazine*, March 2014.

"For a Girl Becoming," *Indigenous Woman*, Summer 2006, vol. VI, no. 1, Austin, TX; *For a Girl Becoming*, University of

Arizona Press, Sun Tracks Series, Tucson, AZ, 2009; *Poetry Speaks, Who I Am*, edited by Elise Paschen, Sourcebooks, Naperville, IL, 2010.

"My friend Sarita" story, Sarita London. Used by permission of storyteller.

"Equinox," *How We Became Human: New and Selected Poems*, W. W. Norton, NY, 2004; http://www.molossus.co/worldpoetryportfolio/world-poetry-portfolio-36-joy-harjo/; http://www.thedrunkenboat.com/harjo.html.

"Sunrise," http://www.molossus.co/worldpoetryportfolio/world-poetry-portfolio-36-joy-harjo/.

Mvto/thank you to so many who have been a part of the endeavor of this book, this song:

Candyce Childers, Pam Uschuk, Gayle Elliot, Sandra Cisneros, Rainy Ortiz, Sarita London, Jill Bialosky, Alison Granucci, Laura Coltelli, Christina Burke, Eli Grayson, Dana Tiger, Dunya Mikhail, Elise Paschen, Jennifer Elizabeth Kreisberg, LeAnne Howe, dg nanouk okpik, Norman Patrick Brown, Selby Minner and the Oklahoma Blues Hall of Fame, the Oklahoma Jazz Hall of Fame, and especially those who take care of *Oce Vpofv*, my granddaughters Haleigh Sarah Bush and Desiray Kierra Chee who carry it on, my Owen, and for all the Holy Beings who have inspired and continue to inspire.

In memory of Patsy Mae Jojola and Charlie Hill.

And with thanks to Adolphe Sax for inventing the saxophone.

I am sitting in the dark.
In the dark I am sitting . . .
without singing any sort of song
. . . without singing I wouldn't be able to talk . . .
now all I can do is wait, wait for the sun
wait for the birds to sing, and all that
may happen when the sun comes up . . .
I am sitting in the dark. In the dark I am sitting.

—DESIRAY CHEE

The sound of cicadas as I lay here waiting for
sleep is drumming in my head . . . A sound that
isn't here in this part of the world, but a sound I
carried with me from home. Home. I miss home.

—HALEIGH SARAH BUSH

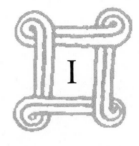

HOW IT CAME TO BE

Only the Indian people are the original people of America. Our roots are buried deep in the soils of America. We are the only people who have continued with the oldest beliefs of this country. We are the people who still yet speak the languages given to us by the Creator.

This is our homeland. We came from no other country.

We have always looked at ourselves as human beings . . .

Every tribe has a trail of tears. We wonder when it is going to end.

PHILLIP DEERE (1929–1985)

I lay my body down in another city, another hotel room. Once Louis Armstrong and his band stayed here. Later the hotel fell to trash. New money resurrected it. Under the red moon of justice, I dream with the king of jazz.

For Calling the Spirit Back from Wandering the Earth in Its Human Feet

Put down that bag of potato chips, that white bread, that bottle of pop.

Turn off that cellphone, computer, and remote control.

Open the door, then close it behind you.

Take a breath offered by friendly winds. They travel the earth gathering essences of plants to clean.

Give it back with gratitude.

If you sing it will give your spirit lift to fly to the stars' ears and back.

Acknowledge this earth who has cared for you since you were a dream planting itself precisely within your parents' desire.

Let your moccasin feet take you to the encampment of the guardians who have known you before time, who will be there after time. They sit before the fire that has been there without time.

Let the earth stabilize your postcolonial insecure jitters.

Be respectful of the small insects, birds and animal people
who accompany you.
Ask their forgiveness for the harm we humans have brought
down upon them.

Don't worry.
The heart knows the way though there may be high-rises,
interstates, checkpoints, armed soldiers, massacres, wars, and
those who will despise you because they despise themselves.

The journey might take you a few hours, a day, a year, a few
years, a hundred, a thousand or even more.

Watch your mind. Without training it might run away and
leave your heart for the immense human feast set by the
thieves of time.

Do not hold regrets.

When you find your way to the circle, to the fire kept burning
by the keepers of your soul, you will be welcomed.

You must clean yourself with cedar, sage, or other healing plant.

Cut the ties you have to failure and shame.

Let go the pain you are holding in your mind, your shoulders,
your heart, all the way to your feet. Let go the pain of your

ancestors to make way for those who are heading in our direction.

Ask for forgiveness.

Call upon the help of those who love you. These helpers take many forms: animal, element, bird, angel, saint, stone, or ancestor.

Call your spirit back. It may be caught in corners and creases of shame, judgment, and human abuse.

You must call in a way that your spirit will want to return. Speak to it as you would to a beloved child.

Welcome your spirit back from its wandering. It may return in pieces, in tatters. Gather them together. They will be happy to be found after being lost for so long.

Your spirit will need to sleep awhile after it is bathed and given clean clothes.

Now you can have a party. Invite everyone you know who loves and supports you. Keep room for those who have no place else to go.

Make a giveaway, and remember, keep the speeches short.

Then, you must do this: help the next person find their way through the dark.

For any spark to make a song it must be transformed by pressure. There must be unspeakable need, muscle of belief, and wild, unknowable elements. I am singing a song that can only be born after losing a country.

Rabbit Is Up to Tricks

In a world long before this one, there was enough for
  everyone,
Until somebody got out of line.
We heard it was Rabbit, fooling around with clay and the
  wind.
Everybody was tired of his tricks and no one would play
  with him;
He was lonely in this world.
So Rabbit thought to make a person.
And when he blew into the mouth of that crude figure to see
What would happen,
The clay man stood up.
Rabbit showed the clay man how to steal a chicken.
The clay man obeyed.
Then Rabbit showed him how to steal corn.
The clay man obeyed.
Then he showed him how to steal someone else's wife.
The clay man obeyed.
Rabbit felt important and powerful.
The clay man felt important and powerful.
And once that clay man started he could not stop.
Once he took that chicken he wanted all the chickens.
And once he took that corn he wanted all the corn.
And once he took that wife, he wanted all the wives.
He was insatiable.

Then he had a taste of gold and he wanted all the gold.
Then it was land and anything else he saw.
His wanting only made him want more.
Soon it was countries, and then it was trade.
The wanting infected the earth.
We lost track of the purpose and reason for life.
We began to forget our songs. We forgot our stories.
We could no longer see or hear our ancestors,
Or talk with each other across the kitchen table.
Forests were being mowed down all over the world.
And Rabbit had no place to play.
Rabbit's trick had backfired.
Rabbit tried to call the clay man back,
But when the clay man wouldn't listen
Rabbit realized he'd made a clay man with no ears.

Listened to an alto sax player jamming on the street. He played a few jazz standards, mostly popular tunes the people would know who changed buses there. Nice tone. I walked from the hotel into the dusk of the city to listen closer, to speak with him. We shared names, gear info, and other stories of the saxophone road. He told me, "I'm making a living out of small hopes . . ." There's something about a lone horn player blowing ballads at the corners of our lives.

No

Yes, that was me you saw shaking with bravery, with a
government-issued rifle on my back. I'm sorry I could not
greet you, as you deserved, my relative.

They were not my tears. I have a reservoir inside. They will
be cried by my sons, my daughters if I can't learn how to
turn tears to stone.

Yes, that was me, standing in the back door of the house in
the alley, with fresh corn and bread for the neighbors.

I did not foresee the flood of blood. How they would forget
our friendship, would return to kill the babies and me.

Yes, that was me whirling on the dance floor. We made such
a racket with all that joy. I loved the whole world in that silly
music.

I did not realize the terrible dance in the staccato of bullets.

Yes. I smelled the burning grease of corpses. And like a fool
I expected our words might rise up and jam the artillery in
the hands of dictators.

We had to keep going. We sang our grief to clean the air of turbulent spirits.

Yes, I did see the terrible black clouds as I cooked dinner. And the messages of the dying spelled there in the ashy sunset. Every one addressed: "mother."

There was nothing about it in the news. Everything was the same. Unemployment was up. Another queen crowned with flowers. Then there were the sports scores.

Yes, the distance was great between your country and mine. Yet our children played in the path between our houses.

No. We had no quarrel with each other.

Humans were created by mistake. Someone laughed and we came crawling out. That was the beginning of the story; we were hooked then. What a wild dilemma, how to make it to the stars, on a highway slick with fear—

Once the World Was Perfect

Once the world was perfect, and we were happy in that
  world.
Then we took it for granted.
Discontent began a small rumble in the earthly mind.
Then Doubt pushed through with its spiked head.
And once Doubt ruptured the web,
All manner of demon thoughts
Jumped through—
We destroyed the world we had been given
For inspiration, for life—
Each stone of jealousy, each stone
Of fear, greed, envy, and hatred, put out the light.
No one was without a stone in his or her hand.
There we were,
Right back where we had started.
We were bumping into each other
In the dark.
And now we had no place to live, since we didn't know
How to live with each other.
Then one of the stumbling ones took pity on another
And shared a blanket.
A spark of kindness made a light.
The light made an opening in the darkness.
Everyone worked together to make a ladder.
A Wind Clan person climbed out first into the next world,

And then the other clans, the children of those clans, their
    children,
And their children, all the way through time—
To now, into this morning light to you.

When I woke up from a forty-year sleep, it was by a song. I could hear the drums in the village. I felt the sweat of ancestors in each palm. The singers were singing the world into place, even as it continued to fall apart. They were making songs to turn hatred into love.

Cricket Song

Tonight I catch a cricket song.
Sung by a cricket who wants the attention of another—
My thinking slides in the wake of the cricket's sweet
Longing. It's lit by the full moon as it makes a path
Over the slick grass of the whitest dark,
I doubt the cricket cares his singing is swinging starlight
To the worry that has darkened my mind.
It is mating season.
They will find their way to each other by sound.
Time and *how* are the mysterious elements of any life.
I will find my way home to you.

MVSKOKE NATION, JUNE 23, 2013

After years you realize that your enemies are as familiar as your friends. You always encounter them in the world. Circumstances continue to pull you together even as you continue to pull apart. Sometimes you are forced by community laws to invite them to sit with you and eat. You are no fool. You make sure when they leave they take only what belongs to them.

Entering the Principality of O'ahu by Sky Roads

Somebody sang these clouds into being.
Tell me, who is your singer?

Does the song maker inhabit the story of the pig god digging
Cliffs, with an angry, passionate love?

Or sing knowledge beneath the misty cloak perched on the
Shoulders of the island spirit?

I want to know this song maker,
Who continues to make songs that lift the most humble
    spirits
To the grass houses of the heavens—

Songs that aren't paid for
By the money and influence
Of rich, fat corporate gods.

Each human is a complex, contradictory story. Some stories within us have been unfolding for years, others are trembling with fresh life as they peek above the horizon. Each is a zigzag of emotional design and ancestral architecture. All the stories in the earth's mind are connected.

We Were There When Jazz
Was Invented

I have lived 19,404 midnights, some of them in the quaver of
fish dreams
And some without any memory at all, just the flash of the
jump
From a night rainbow, to an island of fire and flowers—such
a holy
Leap between forgetting and jazz. How long has it been
since I called you back?
After Albuquerque with my baby in diapers on my hip; it
was a difficult birth,
I was just past girlhood slammed into motherhood. What a
bear.

Beyond the door of my tongue is a rail and I'm leaning over
to watch bears
Catch salmon in their teeth. That realm isn't anywhere near
Los Angeles. If I dream
It all back then I reconstruct that song buried in the muscle
of urgency. I'm bereft
In the lost nation of debtors. Wey yo hey, wey yo hey yah
hey. Pepper jumped
And some of us went with him to the stomp. All night,
beyond midnight, back
Up into the sky, holy.

It was a holy mess, wholly of our folly, drawn of ashes
   around the hole
Of our undoing. Back there the ceremonial fire was
   disassembled, broken and bare, like chord breaks
   forgetting to blossom. Around midnight, I turn my back
And watch prayers take root beneath the moon. Not that
   dreams
Have anything to do with it exactly. I get jumpy
In the aftermath of a disturbed music. I carried that baby up
   the river, gave birth

To nothing but the blues in buckskin and silk. Get back, I
   said, and what bird
Have you chosen to follow in your final years of solitude?
   Go ahead, jump holy
Said the bear prophet. Wey ya hah. Wey ya hah. All the way
   down to the jamming
Flowers and potholes. There has to be a saxophone
   somewhere, some notes bear
Little resemblance to the grown child. Now I've got to be
   dreaming.
Take me back

Or don't take me back to Tulsa. I can only marry the music;
   the outlook's bleak
Without it. I mean it. And then I don't. Too many questions
   mar the answer. Breath
Is the one. And two. And. Dream sweet prophet of sound,
   dream
Mvskoke acrobat of disruption. It's nearing midnight and
   something holy

Is always coming around. Take love for instance, and the
  bare
Perfect neck of a woman who's given up everything for the
  forbidden leap

To your arms as you lean over the railing to hear the music
  hopping at the jump
Pull of the line. She will never be here again in the break of
  the phrase back
Before this maverick music was invented. It's the midnight
  hour and sweet dark love bares
It all. I can hear it again; the blue moon caving in to tears of
  muscle and blood. Birth
Of the new day begins less than one second after. It's that
  exact, this science of the holy.
So that's where it is, this incubation of broken dreams.

It took forever for that bear of a horn player to negotiate the
  impossible jump.
Weh yo hey Weh yo hah, those water spirits will carry that
  girl all the way back
To the stomp grounds where jazz was born. It's midnight.
  How holy.

This is only one of many worlds. Worlds are beings,
each with their own themes, rules, and ways of doing.
Humans in this world fall too easily to war, are quick to
take offense, and claim ownership. "What drama," said
crow, dodging traffic as he wrestled a piece of road kill.

Reality Show (song)

Nizhoniigo no hey nay
Nizhoniigo no hey way nay
Nizhoniigo no hey nay
Nizhoniigo no hey way nay

How do we get out of here?
Smoke hole crowded with too much thinking
Too many seers
And prophets of prosperity
We call it real.

What are we doing in this mess of forgetfulness?
Ruled by sharp things, baby girls in stiletto heels
Beloved ones doing street time
We call it real; we call it real.

What are we doing napping, through war?
We've lost our place in the order of kindness
Children are killing children
We call it real.

How do we get out of here?
Smoke hole crowded with too much thinking
Too many seers

And prophets of prosperity
We call it real.

What are we doing forgetting love?
Under mountains of trash, a river on fire
We can't be bought, forced, or destroyed.
Just what is real?

How do we get out of here?
Smoke hole crowded with too much thinking
Too many seers
And prophets of prosperity
We call it real.

Nizhoniigo no hey nay
Nizhoniigo no hey way nay
Nizhoniigo no hey nay
Nizhoniigo no hey way nay

When I blow my horn, I depend on the assistance of the winds. I depend on love. I hear my saxophone ancestors beginning with Lester Young, Ben Webster, John Coltrane to Jim Pepper, and hear the ancient guardian of the grounds calling out in each direction with a conch shell. We are all here, they tell me, still singing about where we have been and where we are going.

Beautiful Baby, Beautiful Child
(a lullaby)

Hokosucē herosē. Estuce herosē.

Beautiful baby, beautiful child.
Hokosucē herosē, Estuce herosē.

The sky is your blanket; the earth is your cradle.
Sutvt vccetv cēnakēt os. Ekvnv cen topv hakes.

Your mother rocks you close to her heart.
Ceckē ēfekkē temposen ce haneces.

Your father holds up the sky.
Cerkē sutv hvlwen kvwapes.

Beautiful baby, beautiful child.
Hokosucē herosē, Estuce herosē.

MVSKOVE TRANSLATION
BY ROSEMARY MCCOMBS MAXEY

II

THE WANDERER

*We are the earth, she told me that day we sat at her
   kitchen table.*
*(Everyone came to her table from the four directions to
   hear her stories.)*
"One day I will be gone," she said.
And what will you remember of what I tell you?"
*I realize now that she was the very Earth herself,
   talking.*

Talking with the Sun

I believe in the sun.
In the tangle of human failures of fear, greed, and
    forgetfulness, the sun gives me clarity.
When explorers first encountered my people, they called us
    heathens, sun worshippers.
They didn't understand that the sun is a relative, and
    illuminates our path on this earth.

After dancing all night in a circle we realize that we are a
    part of a larger sense of stars and planets dancing with us
    overhead.
When the sun rises at the apex of the ceremony, we are
    renewed.
There is no mistaking this connection, though Walmart
    might be just down the road.
Humans are vulnerable and rely on the kindnesses of the
    earth and the sun; we exist together in a sacred field of
    meaning.

Our earth is shifting. We can all see it.
I hear from my Inuit and Yupik relatives up north that
    everything has changed. It's so hot; there is not enough
    winter.
Animals are confused. Ice is melting.

The quantum physicists have it right; they are beginning to
    think like Indians: everything is connected dynamically
    at an intimate level.
When you remember this, then the current wobble of the
    earth makes sense. How much more oil can be drained,
Without replacement; without reciprocity?

I walked out of a hotel room just off Times Square at dawn
    to find the sun.
It was the fourth morning since the birth of my fourth
    granddaughter.
This was the morning I was to present her to the sun, as a
    relative, as one of us. It was still dark, overcast as I walked
    through Times Square.
I stood beneath a twenty-first century totem pole of symbols
    of multinational corporations, made of flash and neon.

The sun rose up over the city but I couldn't see it amidst the
    rain.
Though I was not at home, bundling up the baby to carry
    her outside,
I carried this newborn girl within the cradleboard of my
    heart.
I held her up and presented her to the sun, so she would be
    recognized as a relative,
So that she won't forget this connection, this promise,
So that we all remember, the sacredness of life.

"One way to look at it," he told me one day as I sawed through scales to make muscle for flying, "is that we are all lost, we were already lost the day we were born. In music, we can become tragically and beautifully lost... and found again."

Spirit Walking in the Tundra

All the way to Nome, I trace the shadow of the plane as it
    walks
Over turquoise lakes made by late spring breakup
Of the Bering Sea.
The plane is so heavy with cargo load it vibrates our bones.
Like the pressure made by light cracking ice.

Below I see pockets of marrow where seabirds nest.
Mothers are so protective they will dive humans.

I walk from the tarmac and am met by an old friend.
We drive to the launching place
And see walrus hunters set out toward the sea.
We swing to the summer camps where seal hangs on drying
    frames.
She takes me home.
I watch her son play video games on break from the
    university.

This is what it feels like, says her son, as we walk up tundra,
Toward a herd of musk ox, *when you spirit walk.*
There is a shaking, and then you are in mystery.

Little purple flowers come up from the permafrost.
A newborn musk ox staggers around its mother's legs.

I smell the approach of someone with clean thoughts.
She is wearing designs like flowers, and a fur of ice.
She carries a basket and digging implements.
Her smell is sweet like blossoms coming up through the
  snow.
The spirit of the tundra stands with us, and we collect
  sunlight together,
We are refreshed by small winds.

We do not need history in books to tell us who we are
Or where we come from, I remind him.
Up here, we are near the opening in the Earth's head, the
  place where the spirit leaves and returns.
Up here, the edge between life and death is thinner than
  dried animal bladder.

(FOR ANUQSRAAQ AND QITUVITUAQ)

NOME, ALASKA, 2011

Where we lived, the settlers built their houses. Where we drew fresh water, the oil companies sucked oil. Where deer ran in countless numbers, we have a new mall. Where the healing plants thrived; the river is burning. Now, a fence cuts the road home. Next the sky will be tethered, and we will pay for air.

Mother Field

That night we headed to the bar
My jones was for the music humping through the door.
No stars yet in the ache of the sky, and
A rat hung in the mouth of the fat cat.
Everyone was there in each burrow of booth, including
Spook and the knot of Indian school brats.
It was the end of the week, the end of the line,
We'd drink to that or anything else that made us laugh.

Everyone had a name that could not be spoken.
Every given name harbored an origin story.
There was no doubt as to the root of the matter.
Spook got his name on the street,
Nez from an ancestor tall as male rain,
And mine was from a grandfather who fought without
     thought
To return us back rightfully to our beloved homelands.

In this bar, we traded despair for disco dance vision, made
     art of trouble,
While boxcars filled with uranium slid up and down
The king's highway along the rushing, shallow river; the
     yellow chaos
Metal made us sick and downward mental.

It was all about a Saturday night at the Senate Lounge
Which wasn't the senate and there was no lounging

I promised Spook I'd never forget him.
He forgot me instead. Ayyyeee.
Nez found God then forgot where she had left him.
And this was only the beginning of the evening.

I left my seat to dance and found it taken over by another.
We'd never seen her here at ground zero of the city, but
We'd all heard the story of her killed lover: Silkwood,
Chased down and killed by the monster Cur-Muggy.

She told us the story as she checked the door, sporadic.
Beneath our bent heads we made a listening temple.
She could not stop to rest or they would get her.
We would all die, she prophesied, of a multi-corporate army,
Of suits in boardrooms who paid workers nothing to do the dirty.

By closing, we were all a state or two from madness.
Everyone was making moves, or begging rides for the next crazy
    party.
The DJ took a breather, as he packed it up for another hard-up
    city.

We offered her refuge; instead, she fled.
She only took what she could carry.
I don't remember her name, or what compelled me to forget
So drenched that night we all were from tough knowledge
Spilling out across the dark earth
In this vulnerable, pulsing mother field.

Let's not shame our eyes for seeing. Instead, thank them for their bravery.

Walk

Dead umbrella—broken wings
Carryout Styrofoam—chicken grease
Crow rain—orange peel in beak.
Blue wad of gum—one day I will sleep.
Ferns drinking rain—I am thirsty for sun.
Winds from up north—lounge here in this mist.
Black squirrel on a slag of stone—carry me home.
Giant tree roots are highway of ant trade routes—where do
    I belong?
Crisp holly with red berries—we are holy with hope.
Another dead umbrella—we are all getting wet.
Winds' cousins—fly up behind them.
Clouds slip to earth—
All this walking and I'm not getting far.
Water spirit feeling . . . round my head—
Where will I go when I am dead?

VANCOUVER, BC

Midnight is a horn player warmed up tight for the last set. One a.m. is a drummer who knows how to lay it sweet. Two a.m. is a guitar player who is down on his luck. Three a.m. is a bass player walking the floor crazy for you. Four a.m. is a singer in silk who will do anything for love. Five a.m. is kept for the birds. Six a.m. is the cleaning crew smoking cigarettes while they wait for the door to open. Seven a.m. we're having breakfast together at the diner that never closes. Eight a.m. and we shut it down, though the clock keeps running, all through the town.

Charlie and the Baby

Charlie was in Venice, wheeling his granddaughter in a
   stroller
Down the boardwalk, through noisy spring crowds.
He was the happiest he'd ever been. He was with the baby,
The sun, and the ocean who busied herself carrying time
And breaking it against sand.

In the sky over Charlie and the baby were flights coming in
   from Hawaii, China, and other lands.
They circled like reachable stars.
Men fished from the pier; mothers unfolded picnics,
As children played hide-and-seek.
In the blue breathed immense light beings.
From their eyes, we were lost and small.

Charlie called and asked me how I was doing—

I probably recited the usual, you know: I am living a life
That takes me almost everywhere. Jet lag. Band practice.
   The kids. Poems.

Charlie was weary with the poverty of making a living of
   comedy.
(We laughed.)
I could smell sea-riding wind, could hear the baby's laughter.

New plants were growing from the grief of my mother's
   recent death.
(We listened.)
As for poets, I said, it's about the same.

We talked what we always talked:
History, saxophones, kids, words, Floyd, Buffy, Jennifer Jesus,
   healing, airplanes, Floyd, prayers, philosophy, Indians,
   Indians, and why we're in the predicament we're in.

Every word that's ever said tries to find a way to live.

You're gone now, and I'm still in this predicament called
   living, Charlie.
I imagine things don't change much when you cross the line.
You're still you.
And I'm still here at the other end of this long, long wave,
   listening.

When I walk over to join you in the two-step, you'd
better say yes the old woman told Death. Death
laughed. For her, death was a fine-looking native man.
He wore old-style buckskin. She took his arm. He was a
good dancer. They two-stepped all the way to the end of
the circle of this earth fire.

Had-It-Up-to-Here Round Dance
(for two voices) with Charlie Hill

Way-ya-ha-yah, way-ya-ha-ya
Way-ya-ha-yah, way-ya-ha-ya-ho

I don't like your girlfriend and her high-heeled shoes
And her skirt up to here
And her blonde hair down to there
When you dance right past with her it gives me the blues
You have the sweetest step in double time it's just not fair
How can I tell you that I love you when you don't even
    care—

I don't like your boyfriend and his white man ways.
You hold him in your shawl it makes me crazed
I like the way you step so high beside me
But how can I tell you babe when you don't talk to me

Way-ya-ha-ya, way-ya-ha-yo

You used to dance, you'd step so high . . .
We used to come to this place all the time because everybody
    knew you
Now it seems like too many people know you here
Now how can I tell you these things, you don't even talk to me

anymore, you don't even call me up anymore, you don't look
at me anymore, you don't even see me anymore—
But if you come close to me I'll tell you how much I love you
honey, how much I love you honey hi yah

I don't like your girlfriend

But

I never liked any of your girlfriends

But

None of them

But

Not your Sioux
Not your Comanche sweetheart

But

Not your shining Shoshone

But

Not your get-down Dineh
Not your too-fast girlfriend

But but

Not your too-fast girlfriend with her um up to here and her
     uh down to there
Her here down . . .

But but

To everywhere, it looks bad on me
How could you do this to me?

Are you done?
Man

Just just just just dance
Get down Get funky
Get down, Get Creek

Way-ya-ha-ya, way-ya-ha-yo

If you come close to me honey hey yah
If you come close to me honey hi yah
I will have to tell you
I will have to tell you
How much I love you, honey . . .

Are you done? Jeesh
Too much
Went out for a couple of drinks
Party
A couple of smokes
Not enough
It didn't mean anything

Rent
I mean, I mean . . .
Not enough
I woke up on the floor with her
Uptime, too much
With my arms around her, but she
Downtime, too much
Passed out, and I was just trying to see if she was
Downtime
If she was still breathing
Runaround
You read things into it
Man . . .

"Through these doors walk some of the finest people in the world," read the sign over that Indian bar in downtown Albuquerque. The dance floor was always packed with a sea of cowboy hats. They made a felt sky. We'd head out before last call, before the fights. We drove up to the cliffs in a pack—to sing all night at the Forty-Nine. We were those fine people, just a little lonely for home.

One Day There Will Be Horses
(a traveling song)

You stood at my door, peered out from the wreck
Of a three-day drunk.
Your eyes said good man, works with hands
And wants a chance.
You wanted a ride to the other side of town.
No way to walk the bridge over Polecat Creek.

One day I will be rich enough
One day I will be lucky enough
One day I will have horses enough to marry with

We talked about relationships, jobs, and all the winners.
You laughed and kicked back
In my truck, in the afternoon sun.
You asked me to let you off near an overpass, north of town.
A creek ran parallel to the highway.
There were trees bending down
To cup the winds.

One day I will be rich enough
One day I will be lucky enough
One day I will have horses enough to marry with

When I looked back, you were walking west
Work shoes and tools over your shoulder.
A little rain began to fall from sparse, lucky clouds.
Did you find a place to sleep?
You light the dark as you sing your traveling song:
One day I will be rich enough
One day I will be lucky enough
One day I will have horses enough to marry with
Hey ya ha, hey ya ho
Hey ya ha, hey ya ho

One day, I will have words enough
One day, I will have songs enough
One day, I will be tough enough
One day, I will have love enough
To go home.

When I returned to my ancestral grounds there stood my relatives welcoming me home. We danced all summer. We visited all the other grounds, sharing food, songs, and nights that made concentric circles of stories on the road to sunrise.

Goin' Home (song)

Last dance and the night is almost over
One last round under the starry sky
We're all going home someway, somehow when it's over
Hey e yah, hey e yay, aye e yah aye e yay

If you've found love in the circle then hold onto it, not too
    tight
If you have to let love go then let it go— Keep on dancing

I don't care if you're married sixteen times
I'll get you yet
Goin' home goin' home

I'm from Oklahoma got no one to call mine
A love supreme, a love supreme
Everybody wants a love supreme

When the dance is over sweetheart, take me home in your
    one-eyed Ford
Or better yet, let's just sit here under the stars wrapped in my
    shawl, and figure out how to get our homelands back—
Goin' home goin' home goin' home

It's time to go home
Be kind to all you meet along the way

Mvto mvto to everybody
For all the good times

Good night, sleep tight
Goin' home, goin' home
Goin' home

Drive safely, or better yet, don't drive at all
Don't forget: hold somebody's hand through the dark.
Goin' home goin' home

Kul-ku-ce cv-na-kē, hv-ya-yi-ca-res
Kul-ku-ce cv-na-kē, hv-ya-yi-ca-res
Kul-ku-ce cv-na-kē, hv-ya-yi-ca-res
Kul-ke-kvs, kul-ke-kvs, kul-ke-kvs

*Our Mvskoke new year is inherently about the
acknowledgment and honoring of the plant world.
We become in harmony with each other. Our worlds
are utterly interdependent. All of our decisions
matter, not just to seven generations and more of
human descendants, but to the seven or more plant
descendants and animal descendants. We make
sacrifices to take care of each other. To understand each
other is profound beyond human words.*

This is what I am singing.

The First Day Without a Mother

In the hour of indigo, between sleeping and wake—
A beloved teacher sits up on the funeral pyre—
He smiles at me through flames that are dancing as they
    eat—
I will see you again, is one of the names for blue—
A color beyond the human sky of mind—
One third up the ladder of blue is where we sit for grief—
I was abandoned by lovers, by ideas that leaped ahead of
    time, and by a father looking for a vision he would never
    find—
Do not leave me again, I want to cry as the blue fire takes my
    teacher.
His ashes cool in my hands.
I'm too proud to let go the tears; they are still in me.
I keep looking back.
Maybe I have turned to salt. It burns blue, like the spirits
    who have already
Started to call me home, up over the last earthy hill broken
    through with starts of blue flowers that heal the wounded
    heart.
Chickadee sings at dawn.
I sit up in the dark drenched in longing.
I am carrying over a thousand names for blue that I didn't
    have at dusk.
How will I feed and care for all of them?

III

VISIONS AND MONSTERS

The politics of politics makes a tricky beast. It destroys either side with equal hand. It has a hunger that never seems to end.

Falling, Falling (song)

One side of me speaks the sacred language of fire
The other part understands in broken heart.

My mind can't make up its crazy mind,
When it's burdened by storm clouds of desire.

Falling, falling
Falling, falling

I didn't want to make the same mistakes.
I had to find my own midnight star.

But when you touch my skin I want back in again.

Falling, falling
Falling, falling

Whiskey Spirit you're not my friend.
Pain in my heart,
Though you call me by
My personal name,
Forget you know me.

Falling, falling
Falling, falling

I looked everywhere for love.
I had no place else to go, but home.

Imagine if we natives went to the cemeteries in your cities and dug up your beloved relatives, pulled off rings, watches, and clothes and called them "artifacts," then carried the bones over to the university for study so we could understand you. Consider that there are more bones of native people in universities and museums for study, than there are those of us living.

In Mystic

My path is a cross of burning trees,
Lit by crows carrying fire in their beaks.
I ask the guardians of these lands for permission to enter.
I am a visitor to this history.
No one remembers to ask anymore, they answer.
What do I expect in this New England seaport town, near
    the birthplace of democracy,
Where I am a ghost?
Even a casino can't make an Indian real.
Or should I say "native," or "savage," or "demon"?
And with what trade language?
I am trading a backwards look for jeopardy.
I agree with the ancient European maps.
There are monsters beyond imagination that troll the waters.
The Puritan's determined ships did fall off the edge of the
    world . . .
I am happy to smell the sea,
Walk the narrow winding streets of shops and restaurants,
    and delight in the company of friends, trees, and small
    winds.
I would rather not speak with history but history came to me.
It was dark before daybreak when the fire sparked.
The men left on a hunt from the Pequot village here where I
    stand.

The women and children left behind were set afire.

I do not want to know this, but my gut knows the language
of bloodshed.

Over six hundred were killed, to establish a home for God's
people, crowed the Puritan leaders in their Sunday
sermons.

And then history was gone in a betrayal of smoke.

There is still burning though we live in a democracy erected
over the burial ground.

This was given to me to speak.

Every poem is an effort at ceremony.

I asked for a way in.

(FOR PAM USCHUK) OCTOBER 31, 2009

*This is the kitchen table university. Everything
you need to know is here. This corn we are serving
embodies lessons in geography, economics, culture,
and colonization. These utensils here tell a story of
materiality and socialization. Salt is about migrations.
Songs are born here to grow food and children. We sing
stories to acknowledge and grow love. Take the blues,
for instance . . .*

Listening to Blues in a Fish Joint, Downtown Denver

I need this unreeling of heartache, and
the downtown turnaround.
—Over, and over and over.
When you gonna come back, baby?
—Over and over and over.
Why did you leave me?
The god of all things reached
Behind the counter, pulled up a sour dishrag and
Cleaned off the mess.
—We all went tumbling down.
I said, over and over and over.
—We all went tumbling down.

I would do anything for you, baby, anything—
I'll take you in my brand-new "per cap" car,
I said, I'll take you anywhere you want to go—
Because together we make a lucky brown bird, a rocking chair, or
An arrow to the sun.

You climbed in that broke-down truck with your old boyfriend
    and took off with him instead.
I would do anything for you, baby, anything
But that—

Indian School Night Song Blues

I call to order the meeting of the girls on restriction at
Indian school.
Locked up in the dorm. We broke the rules.
Now it's Saturday night. No booze, you lose.
Music courtesy of KOMA straight from Oklahoma City
Across the plain of tears and fears, and over the mountains
to here
The City Different, Indian school, hippie crash—
Let's dance. Where's the dorm matron? Hide the stash.

We all admire Marlene; she's one of the best.
She's Jackson Pollock in a dress. She only leaves the painting
studio
For sleep or work, and on Sunday she sneaks out to the
Indian
Hospital on the other side of campus— She took me once.
The children clapped and laughed when she came in.
She brought them gifts: all her desserts saved up for a week:
crayons, paper, and tiny fans. We hid when the staff came
in.
They eventually threw her out.
The hospital carries no insurance to cover the harm she
might do.

And Venus . . . now that's a name, and a history.
One parent from the north on the back of a horse,
The other from the south over the back of a river.
Venus is a singer, a real singer. Each singer has a particular
    gift.
Some grow plants, some call helpers.
Some heal the sick, some make the dead rise up and dance.
When Venus sings we enter into a trance.
We no longer hurt from freak chance.
You're going to make it to Broadway
Either New York or Albuquerque.

Mary, Mary quite contrary you're as silent as a mouse in the
    corner
Of the dining hall, chewing on stale American bread.
We don't know who you are or where you've been, maybe
    you're dead
To this reality. None of us are coping well with the BIA.
We've read the reports:
"Doesn't play well with others," "won't speak or look us in
    the eyes," "talks to ghosts"—
We hear what they are saying: "we have the guns and money,
    and we have your children"—

Mary's spirit is mostly underground, with clay.
When she's with us, she roams the halls in precise
    eyeglasses, bell-bottoms laced tight, and a stack of poetry
    in her arms.
T. S. Eliot, she says, needed to put his hands in clay.
She reads him every day, perched with her books outside the
    powwow circle.

Where's Kip? We can't find her anywhere.
She's not in the laundry room, practicing powwow in her
    underwear.
She's not on the roof where she sneaks her smokes.
She's not in the tent she made of government-issued
    bedspreads
Where she sketches high fashion of Indians in Paris.

Here comes Kip with a knife.
And there she goes. No top or bottom.
Only fury whirling in a spiritual nudity.
She's headed out into the snow.
She's what happens when somebody hurts the baby.

We can corner our sheets so a quarter spins, and know the
    drill
For shots, debugging, and towels.
We have a chance.

Do not feed the monsters.
Some are wandering thought forms, looking for a place
to set up house.
Some are sent to you deliberately. They come from
    arrows of gossip, jealousy or envy—and inadvertently
    from thoughtlessness.
They feed on your attention, and feast on your fear.

Suicide Watch

1.

I was on a train stopped sporadically at checkpoints.
What tribe are you, what nation, what race, what sex, what
  unworthy soul?

2.

I could not sleep, because I could not wake up.
No mirror could give me back what I wanted.

3.

I was given a drug to help me sleep.
Then another drug to wake up.
Then a drug was given to me to make me happy.
They all made me sadder.

4.

Death will gamble with anyone.
There are many fools down here who believe they will win.

5.

You know, said my teacher, you can continue to wallow, or
You can stand up here with me in the sunlight and watch the
    battle.

6.

I sat across from a girl whose illness wanted to jump over to
    me.
No! I said, but not aloud.
I would have been taken for crazy.

7.

We will always become those we have ever judged or
    condemned.

8.

This is not mine. It belongs to the soldiers who raped the
young women on the Trail of Tears. It belongs to Andrew
Jackson. It belongs to the missionaries. It belongs to the
thieves of our language. It belongs to the Bureau of Indian
Affairs. It no longer belongs to me.

9.

I became fascinated by the dance of dragonflies over the
   river.
I found myself first there.

We all have helpers in seen and unseen realms.
Give them something to do.
Otherwise, they will grow inattentive with boredom.
They can clean junk from your mind,
Find the opening note for the chorus of a song,
Or give a grandchild a safe path through the dark.
They will not give you winning numbers at the casino,
Wash your dishes, or take out an enemy.
Thank them.
Feed them once in a while.

This Morning I Pray for My Enemies

And whom do I call my enemy?
An enemy must be worthy of engagement.
I turn in the direction of the sun and keep walking.
It's the heart that asks the question, not my furious mind.
The heart is the smaller cousin of the sun.
It sees and knows everything.
It hears the gnashing even as it hears the blessing.
The door to the mind should only open from the heart.
An enemy who gets in, risks the danger of becoming a friend.

"Ah, but what about being on the earth and how we move about the earth?" Gato sang with his horn. And he broke my heart with his longing.

Conflict Resolution for Holy Beings

*I am the holy being of my mother's prayer and
my father's song.*

DINEH POET AND SPEAKER

1. SET CONFLICT RESOLUTION GROUND RULES:

Recognize whose lands these are on which we stand.
Ask the deer, turtle, and the crane.
Make sure the spirits of these lands are respected and
    treated with goodwill.
The land is a being who remembers everything.
You will have to answer to your children, and their children,
    and theirs—
The red shimmer of remembering will compel you up the
    night to walk the perimeter of truth for understanding.
As I brushed my hair over the hotel sink to get ready I heard:
By listening we will understand who we are in this holy
    realm of words.
Do not parade, pleased with yourself.
You must speak in the language of justice.

2. USE EFFECTIVE COMMUNICATION SKILLS THAT DISPLAY AND ENHANCE MUTUAL TRUST AND RESPECT:

If you sign this paper we will become brothers. We will no longer fight. We will give you this land and these waters "as long as the grass shall grow and the rivers run."

The lands and waters they gave us did not belong to them to give. Under false pretenses we signed. After drugging by drink, we signed. With a mass of gunpower pointed at us, we signed. With a flotilla of war ships at our shores, we signed. We are still signing. We have found no peace in this act of signing.

A casino was raised up over the gravesite of our ancestors. Our own distant cousins pulled up the bones of grandparents, parents, and grandchildren from their last sleeping place. They had forgotten how to be human beings. Restless winds emerged from the earth when the graves were open and the winds went looking for justice.

If you raise this white flag of peace, we will honor it.

At Sand Creek several hundred women, children, and men were slaughtered in an unspeakable massacre, after a white flag was raised. The American soldiers trampled the white flag in the blood of the peacemakers.

There is a suicide epidemic among native children. It is triple the rate of the rest of America. "It feels like wartime," said a child welfare worker in South Dakota.

If you send your children to our schools we will train them to get along in this changing world. We will educate them.

We had no choice. They took our children. Some ran away and froze to death. If they were found they were dragged back to the school and punished. They cut their hair, took away their language, until they became as strangers to themselves even as they became strangers to us.

If you sign this paper we will become brothers. We will no longer fight. We will give you this land and these waters in exchange "as long as the grass shall grow and the rivers run."

Put your hand on this bible, this blade, this pen, this oil derrick, this gun and you will gain trust and respect with us. Now we can speak together as one.

We say, put down your papers, your tools of coercion, your false promises, your posture of superiority and sit with us before the fire. We will share food, songs, and stories. We will gather beneath starlight and dance, and rise together at sunrise.

The sun rose over the Potomac this morning, over the city
  surrounding the white house.
It blazed scarlet, a fire opening truth.

White House, or *Chogo Hvtke*, means the house of the
   peacekeeper, the keepers of justice.
We have crossed this river to speak to the white leader for
   peace many times
Since these settlers first arrived in our territory and made
   this their place of governance.
These streets are our old trails, curved to fit around trees.

3. GIVE CONSTRUCTIVE FEEDBACK:

We speak together with this trade language of English. This trade language enables us to speak across many language boundaries. These languages have given us the poets:

Ortiz, Silko, Momaday, Alexie, Diaz, Bird, Woody, Kane, Bitsui, Long Soldier, White, Erdrich, Tapahonso, Howe, Louis, Brings Plenty, okpik, Hill, Wood, Maracle, Cisneros, Trask, Hogan, Dunn, Welch, Gould . . .

The 1957 Chevy is unbeatable in style. My broken-down one-eyed Ford will have to do. It holds everyone: Grandma and grandpa, aunties and uncles, the children and the babies, and all my boyfriends. That's what she said, anyway, as she drove off for the Forty-Nine with all of us in that shimmying wreck.

This would be no place to be without blues, jazz—Thank you/*mvto* to the Africans, the Europeans sitting in, especially Adolphe Sax with his saxophones . . . Don't forget that at the center is the Mvskoke ceremonial circles. We know how to swing. We keep the heartbeat of the earth in our stomp dance feet.

You might try dancing theory with a bustle, or a jingle dress, or with turtles strapped around your legs. You might try wearing colonization like a heavy gold chain around a pimp's neck.

4. REDUCE DEFENSIVENESS AND BREAK THE
    DEFENSIVENESS CHAIN:

I could hear the light beings as they entered every cell. Every
cell is a house of the god of light, they said. I could hear the
spirits who love us stomp dancing. They were dancing as
if they were here, and then another level of here, and then
another, until the whole earth and sky was dancing.

We are here dancing, they said. There was no there.

There was no "I" or "you."

There was us; there was "we."

There we were as if we were the music.

You cannot legislate music to lockstep nor can you legislate
the spirit of the music to stop at political boundaries—

—Or poetry, or art, or anything that is of value or matters in
this world, and the next worlds.

This is about getting to know each other.

We will wind up back at the blues standing on the edge of
the flatted fifth about to jump into a fierce understanding
together.

5. ELIMINATE NEGATIVE ATTITUDES DURING
   CONFLICT:

A panther poised in the cypress tree about to jump is a
panther poised in a cypress tree about to jump.

The panther is a poem of fire green eyes and a heart charged
by four winds of four directions.

The panther hears everything in the dark: the unspoken
tears of a few hundred human years, storms that will break
what has broken his world, a bluebird swaying on a branch a
few miles away.

He hears the death song of his approaching prey:

I will always love you, sunrise.
I belong to the black cat with fire green eyes.
There, in the cypress tree near the morning star.

6. AND, USE WHAT YOU LEARN TO RESOLVE
   YOUR OWN CONFLICTS AND TO MEDIATE
   OTHERS' CONFLICTS:

When we made it back home, back over those curved roads
that wind through the city of peace, we stopped at the
doorway of dusk as it opened to our homelands.
We gave thanks for the story, for all parts of the story
because it was by the light of those challenges we knew
ourselves—
We asked for forgiveness.
We laid down our burdens next to each other.

The first horn I played was a King Super tenor saxophone. My then-lover, a horn player, wrote out the G blues scale for me and I began there, in the heartache of the Americas. In that scale are ships from Africa and Europe. In it are my people dancing in a widening spiral beneath circles of star nebula, giving birth to the swing. I walked up and down the scale, past babies crying in the night for milk, lovers waking in the dawn for more.

Forever (a song)

In the night of memory
There is a mist
In the mist is a house.
It's the heart where we lived.
In that living was a radio.
Guitars played our song.
You'd catch me in your arms
We'd go round and round.

Where does it go, this forever?

Once I was broken by time.
There was no house in the mist.
I lost sunrise. I lost your fire against mine.
A country was falling and falling.
I turned my ears to catch music.
Nothing came back.
No angels of laughter, no you.
I stood alone in the emptiness of memory
Forever and ever—

Where does it go, this forever?

And what about sorrow? I asked time.
Time had nothing to say.
It walked away.

Where does it go, this forever?

I crossed time to the house in the mist.
It's not any house; it's the heart where we live.
In that living is a radio.
There are guitars, a bass, some drums and a horn.
They play our song.
You catch me in your arms and we go round and round.
We are laughter and flying.
We are fire and wet.
In this time we live forever.
And ever and ever.

And then I argued with myself. —You can't say
everything, what will he think of you? Besides, to speak
everything is to exhaust mystery.

I Am Not Ready to Die Yet

My death peers at the world through a *plumeria* tree
The tree looks out over the neighbor's house to the Pacific
A blue water spirit commands this part of the earth mind
Without question, it rules from the kingdom of secrets
And tremendous fishes.

I was once given to the water.
My ashes will return there,
But I am not ready to die yet—

This morning I carry the desire to live, inside my thigh
It pulses there: a banyan, a mynah bird, or a young impatient
    wind
Until I am ready to fly again, over the pungent flowers
Over the sawing and drilling workmen making a mess
In the yard of the house next door—

It is endless, this map of eternity.

Beware the water monster that lives at the borders of
    doubt—
He can swallow everything whole: all the delectable
    mangoes, dreams, and even the most faithful of planets—

I was once given to the water.
My ashes will return there,
But I am not ready to die yet—

And when it happens, as it certainly will, the lights
Will go on in the city and the city will go on shining
At the edge of the water—it is endless—this earthy mind—

There will be flowers. There are always flowers,
And a fine blessing rain will fall through the net of the
    clouds
Bearing offerings to the stones, and to all who linger.

It will be a day like any other.
Someone will be hammering; someone will be frying fish.
And at noon the workmen will go home
to eat poi, pork, and rice.

Whenever a saxophone begins to sing in a story we know that for a time, we will no longer move about so lonely here, far away from the house of the sun, moon, and stars.

Report from the Edge of a Terrible Regime

The sky aches with primordial dark
As it prepares to give birth to light—

—A chuk-chuk of gecko song—

And a young trade wind follows another
Through the screened house over
The green mountain ridge who wears a cape of clouds.

Down the hill in Chinatown
A sailor sodden with drink and fight
Zips up from a piss.
He curses everything he stumbles against
In the flower ruins.

One god breaks against another.
And so it is.

In one house lives the sun, moon, and stars. Within that house is another house of sun, moon, and stars. —And then another, and another— There is no end to the imagination.

From DFW Airport at Dawn

The final drift of *pikake* blesses the departure
Then I'm gone
Over the islands of fire and green, I fly east
Over the houses on the ridge of the heavens, I fly east
Over the mango tree, banana trees, and years of sunrises
    and sunsets, I fly east
Over the canoes racing to shore in a great commotion,
    I fly east
This poem is a blessing for those I have left behind
And for that which I can never leave behind—

What kept me going was that perfect song I kept hearing, just beyond the field of perceptible sound. I palpitated it, as my breath attempted to make the horn into a living being.

The Last World of Fire and Trash (song)

I don't know anything anymore
or if that cricket is still singing
in a country where crickets are banned.

I'm Indian in a strange pastiche of hurt and rain
smells like curry and sweat
from a sunset rock-and-roll restaurant.
A familiar demon groaning with fear has stalked me here,
ruins poetry, then his swollen pride commandeers.

Beneath the moon rocking above Los Angeles
or outside the stomp dance fire of memory,
I told him, you can choose to hate me
for going too far, or for being a nothing
next to a pretty nothing like you.

So long, goodbye, oh fearful one.
My desires had turned into a small mountain.
Of dirty clothes, sax gig bag, guitar
books, shoes, and grief
that I packed and carried
from one raw wound to another.

I can't get betrayal out of my heart,
out of my mind

in this hotel room where I'm packing for home.
I've seen that same face whirring
in the blur of a glass of wine
after the crashed dance,
the goodbye song
in the last world of fire and trash.

The most dangerous demons spring from fire
and a broken heart, smell of bittersweet aftershave
and the musk of a thousand angels.
And then I let that thought go running away
because I refuse to stay in bondage
to an enemy, who thinks he wants what I have.

I turned my cheek as my head parted through a curtain of
    truth
and erupted from the spirit world to this gambling place—
So I send prayers skyward on smoke.
Hvsaketvmese, Hvsaketvmese.
Release this suffering.
May the pretty beast and all the world know peace.

I refuse to sum it up anymore; it's not possible.
I give it up
to the battering of songs against the light,
to the singing of the earnest cricket
in the last world of fire and trash.

THE WORLD

The poetry ancestors scattered to all parts of the world.
Each family of trees, animals, winds, stones needed a poet.

You Can Change the Story, My Spirit Said to Me as I Sat Near the Sea

FOR SHARON OARD WARNER AND DG NANOUK OKPIK

I am in a village up north, in the lands named "Alaska" now. These places had their own names long before English, Russian, or any other politically imposed trade language.

It is in the times when people dreamed and thought together as one being. That doesn't mean there weren't individuals. In those times, people were more individual in personhood than they are now in their common assertion of individuality: one person kept residence on the moon even while living in the village. Another was a man who dressed up and lived as a woman and was known as the best seamstress.

I have traveled to this village with a close friend who is also a distant relative. We are related to nearly everyone by marriage, clan, or blood.

The first night after our arrival, a woman is brutally killed in the village. Murder is not commonplace. The evil of it puts the whole village at risk. It has to be dealt with immediately so that the turbulence will not leave the people open to more evil.

Because my friend and I are the most obvious influence, it is decided that we are to be killed, to satisfy the murder, to ensure the village will continue in a harmonious manner. No one tells us we are going to be killed. We know it; my bones know it. It is unfortunate, but it is how things must be.

The next morning, my friend and I have walked down from the village to help gather, when we hear the killing committee coming for us.
I can hear them behind us, with their implements and stones, in their psychic roar of purpose.
I know they are going to kill us. I thank the body that has been my clothing on this journey. It has served me well for protection and enjoyment.
I hear—I still hear—the crunch of bones as the village mob, sent to do this job, slams us violently. It's not personal for most of them. A few gain pleasure.
I feel my body's confused and terrible protest, then my spirit leaps out above the scene and I watch briefly before circling toward the sea.

I linger out over the sea, and my soul's helper who has been with me through the stories of my being says, "You can go back and change the story."

My first thought was, *Why would I want to do that? I am free of the needs of earth existence. I can move like wind and water.* But then, because I am human, not bird or whale, I feel compelled.
"What do you mean, 'change the story'?"

Then I am back in the clothes of my body outside the village. I am back in the time between the killing in the village and my certain death in retribution.

"Now what am I supposed to do?" I ask my Spirit. I can see no other way to proceed through the story.

My Spirit responds, "You know what to do. Look, and you will see the story."

And then I am alone with the sea and the sky. I give my thinking to time and let them go play.

It is then I see. I see a man in the village stalk a woman. She is not interested in him, but he won't let go. He stalks her as he stalks a walrus. He is the village's best hunter of walrus. He stalks her to her home, and when no one else is there, he trusses her as if she were a walrus, kills her and drags her body out of her house to the sea. I can see the trail of blood behind them. I can see his footprints in blood as he returns to the village alone.

I am in the village with my friend. The people are gathering and talking about the killing. I can feel their nudges toward my friend and I. I stand up with a drum in my hand. I say:

"I have a story I want to tell you."

And then I begin drumming and dancing to accompany the story. It is pleasing, and the people want to hear more.

They want to hear what kind of story I am bringing from my village.

I sing, dance, and tell the story of a walrus hunter. He is the best walrus hunter of a village. I sing about his relationship to the walrus, and how he has fed his people. And how skilled he is as he walks out onto the ice to call out the walrus.

And then I tell the story of the killing of a walrus who is like a woman. I talk about the qualities of the woman, whom the man sees as a walrus. By now, the story has its own spirit that wants to live. It dances and sings and breathes. It surprises me with what it knows.

With the last step, the last hit of the drum, the killer stands up, as if to flee the gathering. The people turn together as one and see him. They see that he has killed the woman, and it is his life that must be taken to satisfy the murder.

When I return to present earth time, I can still hear the singing.
I get up from my bed and dance and sing the story.
It is still in my tongue, my body, as if it has lived there all along,
though I am in a city with many streams of peoples from far and wide across the earth.

We make a jumble of stories. We do not dream together.

Those who could see into the future predicted the storm long before the first settler stepped on the shores of the Mvskoke story. What was known in both worlds broke. In jazz, a break takes you to the skinned-down bones. You stop for a moment and bop through the opening, then keep playing to the other side of a dark and heavy history.

Sunrise Healing Song

Shining persons arrive here
Ha yut ke lani
Open your being
Ha yut ke jate
In every small thought of what to fix
In every immense thought of dancers winding through the
    Milky Way
Ha yut ke lvste
What obscures, falls away.
Ha yut ke hvtke

I knew there was no way we get out of there when I heard the first cannon shot fired over the ramparts we'd built of logs. I knew it was over for this part of the story. I smelled blood even before the musket hole.

It's Raining in Honolulu

There is a small mist at the brow of the mountain,

Each leaf of flower, of taro, tree, and bush shivers with
ecstasy.

And the rain songs of all the flowering ones who have called
for the rain

Can be found there, flourishing beneath the currents of
singing.

Rain opens us, like flowers, or earth that has been thirsty for
more than a season.

We stop all of our talking, quit thinking, to drink the
mystery.

We listen to the breathing beneath our breathing.

We hear how the rain became rain, how we became human.

The wetness saturates and cleans everything, including the
perpetrators

Of the second overthrow.

We will plant songs where there were curses.

The day went on as it always had, though we fought the government's troops in that crook of the river that had given us much pleasure. The sun kept moving, as did the clouds. The birds were however silent. They could not comprehend the violence of humans.

Praise the Rain

Praise the rain, the seagull dive
The curl of plant, the raven talk—
Praise the hurt, the house slack
The stand of trees, the dignity—
Praise the dark, the moon cradle
The sky fall, the bear sleep—
Praise the mist, the warrior name
The earth eclipse, the fired leap—
Praise the backwards, upward sky
The baby cry, the spirit food—
Praise canoe, the fish rush
The hole for frog, the upside-down—
Praise the day, the cloud cup
The mind flat, forget it all—

Praise crazy. Praise sad.
Praise the path on which we're led.
Praise the roads on earth and water.
Praise the eater and the eaten.
Praise beginnings; praise the end.
Praise the song and praise the singer.

Praise the rain; it brings more rain.
Praise the rain; it brings more rain.

Time is a being, like you, like me. Monahwee made friends with time, shared tobacco with time, so when he got on his horse to race his beloved warrior friends he had a little talk with time. Time said, "Get on my back, and we'll fly free." No matter how fast all the others raced, Monahwee and his horse always arrived long before it was possible . . . those were the best times.

Rushing the Pali

There's not enough time,
no *puka* to squeeze through
the head, then the shoulder
then the rest of it:
a poem
with hands, feet, and
a mysterious heart.
It's too late.
I've promised a ride
to hula, and then
I am to paddle an outrigger
to *Kewalo*
and back in sprint time.
There is holy woven
even in the rush
where can be found
mythic roots for example how
this island was formed
from desire and fire
from the bottom of the sea
to the heavens,
and how humans came to be
next to the trees
who are teased by *kalohe* winds
who travel wild

from one side of the island
to the other.
I am attracted
by the curling indigo of the holy,
sea turtles alongside the canoe
in the mist of elegant consciousness
floating above the clatter
of annoyance.
I climbed up dawn with the dancers
of sunrise.
The earth moved
lightly because she was
moved.
I begin climbing down sunset
over the *Pali*
as traffic slowed for a stop,
then the traffic started
all over again.

I thought of all the doors that had opened and closed. I thought of how so many I loved were no longer on this earth. I thought of all of my mother's songs looking for a place to live. I thought of all the Saturdays in the world. I started with G and rounded the bend at B flat. I followed my soul.

Surfing Canoes

We've felt the winds surf the waves
Alongside the canoe
This is where joy lives
This moment of earth breath
Lifting up with us
Letting us go with us
One blue circle of bliss following another
Like dolphins leaping
To catch sunrise
Making happiness of water
We flew in that canoe
Through particles of memory
Sea turtles lifting their heads
Catching wind
Their lungs drumming
We lift up from sleep, and you take me in your arms
We head out for another wave
And then another

FOR OWEN

I returned to the city of country swing, square dance, round dance, stomp dance, gospel, hymn, powwow, rock-and-roll, blues, jazz, and rhythm-and-blues. We each carry the story of our birthplace in pieces of earth, water, sky, and spirit. Though nothing much appears to have changed here in this Indian town along the Arkansas River, it is always changing.

Speaking Tree

I had a beautiful dream I was dancing with a tree.
—SANDRA CISNEROS

Some things on this earth are unspeakable:
Genealogy of the broken—
A shy wind threading leaves after a massacre,
Or the smell of coffee and no one there—

Some humans say trees are not sentient beings,
But they do not understand poetry—

Nor can they hear the singing of trees when they are fed by
Wind, or water music—
Or hear their cries of anguish when they are broken and
    bereft—

Now I am a woman longing to be a tree, planted in a moist,
    dark earth
Between sunrise and sunset—

I cannot walk through all realms—
I carry a yearning I cannot bear alone in the dark—

What shall I do with all this heartache?

The deepest-rooted dream of a tree is to walk
Even just a little ways, from the place next to the doorway—
To the edge of the river of life, and drink—

I have heard trees talking, long after the sun has gone down:

Imagine what would it be like to dance close together
In this land of water and knowledge . . .

To drink deep what is undrinkable.

*I heard a raven cry the blues one winter, in Anchorage,
outside the Indian hospital. There was thick snow on
the ground. Bushes with red berries lined the walk to
the entrance. On a light post hunched a raven. He was
mourning his human who was dying inside, who would
be gone by sundown.*

What will I do without you?
*How will I find you again in the woven story of dark
and light?*

Everybody Has a Heartache (a blues)

In the United terminal in Chicago at five on a Friday
    afternoon
The sky is breaking with rain and wind and all the flights
Are delayed forever. We will never get to where we are going
And there's no way back to where we've been.
The sun and the moon have disappeared to an island far
    from anywhere.

Everybody has a heartache—

The immense gatekeeper of Gate Z-100 keeps his cool.
This guardian of the sky teases me and makes me smile
    through the mess,
Building up his airline by stacking it against the company I
    usually travel:
Come on over to our side, we'll treat you nice.
I laugh as he hands me back my ticket, then he turns to
    charm
The next customer, his feet tired in his minimum-wage
    shoes.

Everybody has a heartache—

Everyone's eating fried, sweet, soft, and fat,
While we wait for word in the heart of the scrambled beast.

The sparkle of soda wets the dream core.
That woman over there the color of broth, did what she was
   told.
It's worked out well as can be expected in a world
Where she was no beauty queen and was never seen,
Always in the back of someplace in the back—
She holds the newest baby. He has the croup.
Shush, shush. Go to sleep, my little baby sheepie.
He sits up front of her with his new crop of teeth.

Everybody has a heartache—

The man with his head bobbing to music no one else can
   hear, speaks to no one, but his body does.
Half his liver is swollen with anger; the other half is trying
To apologize—
What a mess I've made of history, he thinks without
   thinking.
Mother coming through the screen door, her clothes torn,
Whimpering: *it's okay baby, please don't cry.*
Don't cry. Baby don't cry.
And he never cries again.

Everybody has a heartache—

Baby girl dressed to impress, toddles about with lace on this
   and ruffle on that—
Her mother's relatives are a few hundred miles away poised
   to welcome.
They might as well live on a planet of ice cream.

She's a brand-new wing, grown up from a family's broken
   hope.
Dance girl, you carry our joy.
Just don't look down.

Everybody has a heartache—

Good-looking punk girl taps this on her screen
to a stranger she has never seen:

Just before dawn, you're high again beneath a breaking sky,
I was slick fine leather with a drink in my hand.
Flying with a comet messenger nobody sees.
The quick visitor predicts that the top will be the bottom
And the bottom will flatten and dive into the sea.

I want to tell her:
You will dine with the lobster king, and
You will dance with crabs clicking castanets. You will sleep
Walk beyond the vestibule of sadness with a stranger
You have loved for years.

Everybody has a heartache—

This silence in the noise of the terminal is a mountain of
   bison skulls.
Nobody knows, nobody sees—
Unless the indigenous are dancing powwow all decked out
   in flash and beauty
We just don't exist. We've been dispersed to an outlaw
   cowboy tale.

What were they thinking with all those guns and those
    handcuffs
In a size for babies?
They just don't choose to remember.
We're here.

In the terminal of stopped time I went unsteady to the beat,
Driven by a hungry spirit who is drunk with words and
    songs.
What can I do?
I have to take care of it.
The famished spirit eats fire, poetry, and pain; it only wants
    love.

I argue:

You want love?
Do you even know what it looks like, smells like?

But you cannot argue with hungry spirits.

Everybody has a heartache—

I don't know exactly where I'm going; I only know where
    I've been,
I want to tell the man who sifted through the wreck to find
    us
In the blues shack of disappeared history—
I feel the weight of his heart against my cheek.

His hand is on my back pulling me to him in the dark, to a
  place
No soldiers can reach—

No matter fire leaping through holes in jump time,
No matter earthquake, or the breaking of love spilling over
  the drek of matter
In the ether, stacking one burden
Against the other—

We will all find our way.

We have a heartache.

*Everyone comes into the world with a job to do—I
don't mean working for a company, a corporation—we
were all given gifts to share, even the animals, even the
plants, minerals, clouds ... all beings.*

For a Girl Becoming

That day your spirit came to us rains came in from the
   Pacific to bless.
Clouds peered over the mountains
in response to the singing of medicine plants—
Who danced back and forth in shawls of mist.

Your mother labored there, so young in earthly years
And your father, and all of us who loved you gathered, where
Pollen blew throughout that earthly house to bless.
And horses were running the land, hundreds of them
To accompany you here, to bless.

I wonder what you thought as you paused there in your
   spirit house
Before you entered into the breathing world to be with us?
Were you longing for us, too?
Our relatives in that beloved place dressed you in black hair,
Brown eyes, skin the color of earth, and turned you in this
   direction.
We want you to know that we urgently gathered to welcome
   you here.
We came bearing gifts to celebrate:

From your mother's house we brought: poetry, music,
   medicine makers, stubbornness, beauty, tribal leaders, a
   yard filled with junked cars and the gift of knowing how
   to make them run.
We carried tobacco and cedar, new clothes and joy for you.

And from your father's house came educators, thinkers,
   dreamers, weavers, and mathematical genius.
They carried a cradleboard, hope, white shell, and turquoise
   for you.
We brought blankets to wrap you in, soft beaded moccasins
   of deerskin.

Did you hear us as you traveled from your rainbow house?
We called you with thunder, with singing.
Did you see us as we gathered in the town beneath the
   mountains?
We were dressed in concern and happiness.
We were overwhelmed, as you moved through the weft of
   your mother
Even before you took your first breath, your eyes blinked
   wide open.

Now, breathe.
And when you breathe remember the source of the gift of all
   breathing.
When you walk, remember the source of the gift of all
   walking.

And when you run, remember the source of the gift of all
running.
And when you laugh, remember the source of the gift of all
laughter.
And when you cry, remember the source of the gift of all
tears.
And when you dream, remember the source of the gift of all
dreaming.
And when your heart is broken, remember the source of the
gift of all breaking.
And when your heart is put back together, remember the
source of all putting back together.

Don't forget how you started your journey from that
rainbow house,
How you traveled and will travel through the mountains
and valleys of human tests.

There are treacherous places along the way, but you can
come to us.
There are lakes of tears shimmering sadly there, but you can
come to us.
And valleys without horses or kindnesses, but you can come
to us.
And angry, jealous gods and wayward humans who will
hurt you, but you can come to us.
You will fall, but you will get back up again, because you are
one of us.

And as you travel with us remember this:

Give a drink of water to all who ask, whether they be plant,
    creature, human or helpful spirit;
May you always have clean, fresh water.

Feed your neighbors. Give kind words and assistance
to all you meet along the way—
We are all related in this place—
May you be surrounded with the helpfulness of family and
    good friends.

Grieve with the grieving, share joy with the joyful.
May you build a strong path with beautiful and truthful
    language.

Clean your room.
May you always have a home: a refuge from storm, a
    gathering-place for safety, for comfort.

Bury what needs to be buried.
Laugh easily at yourself; may you always travel lightly and
    well.

Praise and give thanks for each small and large thing.
May you grow in knowledge, in compassion, and beauty.

Always within you is that day your spirit came to us
When rains came in from the ocean to bless

They peered over the mountains in response to the singing
    of medicine plants
Who danced back and forth in shawls of mist.

Your mother labored there, so young in earthly years.
And we who love you gather here,
Pollen blows throughout this desert house to bless.
And horses run the land, hundreds of them for you,
And you are here to bless.

I keep thinking of my boyfriend coming upon some children playing with a fox, just a few blocks down the street. He stopped and got out of the car. It's not every day you see a fox frolicking with children. He asked the children, "Is this your fox?" "No," they told him, "he just came up and started playing with us."

Fall Song

It is a dark fall day.
The earth is slightly damp with rain.
I hear a jay.
The cry is blue.
I have found you in the story again.
Is there another word for "divine"?
I need a song that will keep sky open in my mind.
If I think behind me, I might break.
If I think forward, I lose now.
Forever will be a day like this
Strung perfectly on the necklace of days.
Slightly overcast
Yellow leaves
Your jacket hanging in the hallway
Next to mine.

My friend Sarita went visiting an ill friend. She
stayed with him for a few days, sharing food, stories
. . . to make peace with their unfinished history. One
afternoon, while he slept, she drove to the post office.
She found a parking space in a lot down the street. She
passed a blind man who was tapping the earth with his
cane as she walked up the steps of the post office. When
she came out she walked around the parking lot looking
for her car, but it wasn't there. She returned to the post
office, where stood the blind man. He was looking for
her. He asked her how he could help her. When she
told him her problem he responded, "Take my arm."
The blind man led her directly to her car. He told her,
"See with your heart, not with your eyes." Then he
disappeared.

For Keeps

Sun makes the day new.
Tiny green plants emerge from earth.
Birds are singing the sky into place.
There is nowhere else I want to be but here.
I lean into the rhythm of your heart to see where it will
     take us.
We gallop into a warm, southern wind.
I link my legs to yours and we ride together,
Toward the ancient encampment of our relatives.
Where have you been? they ask.
And what has taken you so long?
That night after eating, singing, and dancing
We lay together under the stars.
We know ourselves to be part of mystery.
It is unspeakable.
It is everlasting.
It is for keeps.

MARCH 4, 2013, CHAMPAIGN, ILLINOIS

I confided in him the longing I was afraid to name. I told him I wrote to leave a trail so that love can find us. I told him that poetry is lonely without the music. I wanted to tell him everything, the way you do when you meet the one who's going to open all the doors in your heart.

Equinox

I must keep from breaking into the story by force,
If I do I will find a war club in my hand
And the smoke of grief staggering toward the sun,
Your nation dead beside you.

I keep walking away though it has been an eternity
And from each drop of blood
Spring up sons and daughters, trees
A mountain of sorrows, of songs.

I tell you this from the dusk of a small city in the north
Not far from the birthplace of cars and industry.
Geese are returning to mate and crocuses have
Broken through the frozen earth.

Soon they will come for me and I will make my stand
Before the jury of destiny. Yes, I will answer in the clatter
Of the new world, I have broken my addiction to war
And desire.
I have buried the dead, and made songs of the blood,
The marrow.

"What are you doing there, soul?" I asked. I felt naked and blown-open without my soul fastened in its usual hidden and dark place.

Sunrise

Sunrise, as you enter the houses of everyone here, find us.
We've been crashing for days, or has it been years.
Find us, beneath the shadow of this yearning mountain,
   crying here.
We have been sick with sour longings, and the jangling of
   fears.
Our spirits rise up in the dark, because they hear,
Doves in cottonwoods calling forth the sun.
We struggled with a monster and lost.
Our bodies were tossed in the pile of kill. We rotted there.
We were ashamed and we told ourselves for a thousand
   years,
We didn't deserve anything but this—
And one day, in relentless eternity, our spirits discerned
   movement of prayers
Carried toward the sun.
And this morning we are able to stand with all the rest
And welcome you here.
We move with the lightness of being, and we will go
Where there's a place for us.